THE LIBRARY OF
HIP-HOP
BIOGRAPHIES™

Ludacris

Philip Wolny

ROSEN
PUBLISHING®

New York

For Océane Dufourg

Published in 2009 by The Rosen Publishing Group, Inc.
29 East 21st Street, New York, NY 10010

Copyright © 2009 by The Rosen Publishing Group, Inc.

First Edition

Library of Congress Cataloging-in-Publication Data

Wolny, Philip.
Ludacris / Philip Wolny.—1st ed.
    p. cm.—(The library of hip-hop biographies)
Includes bibliographical references and index.
ISBN-13: 978-1-4358-5054-5 (library binding)
ISBN-13: 978-1-4358-5440-6 (pbk)
ISBN-13: 978-1-4358-5446-8 (6 pack)
1. Ludacris (Rapper)—Juvenile literature. 2. Rap musicians—United States—Biography—Juvenile literature. I. Title.
ML3930.L85W66 2009
782.421649092—dc22

                                                            2008027302

Manufactured in the United States of America

On the cover: Ludacris performs onstage at the 49th Annual Grammy Awards at the Staples Center in Los Angeles, California, on February 11, 2007, the same night he won a Grammy for Best Album.

CONTENTS

INTRODUCTION

When Christopher Bridges, better known to most of the world as Ludacris, stepped into his old high school in Atlanta, Georgia, in May 2008, he found a face staring back at him: his own. Emblazoned on one wall of the gymnasium of Banneker High School was a mural of him, emblazoned with the words "Gym of Dreams."

Ludacris was just a skinny, undersized kid with big dreams when he started at Banneker. Now he stood, thirty years old, in the Christopher Bridges Gymnasium, a room named for him. He had come to campaign against youth violence and spoke to about two thousand students. According to the Associated Press, he said, "I know a lot of us come from hard times, but it's extremely important that you use your street knowledge and book knowledge to get where you need to be."

Ludacris, who is often referred to simply as "Luda," lives life to the fullest. He's a multiplatinum-selling hip-hop artist, actor, record label owner (of Disturbing tha Peace

Records, or DTP), restaurateur, and philanthropist. But, as many people who know the man behind the outrageous hip-hop persona will tell you, his success has come from hard work and a positive outlook on life.

Ludacris's legendary work ethic started at a young age. He told MTV.com that his first performance was at the age of nine. Indeed, it can often seem as if Ludacris has never rested a day in his life. It is this dedication, along with pure talent, that catapulted him from selling fifty thousand records on his own label to selling millions as the first artist signed to Def Jam South, the famous New York hip-hop label's southern imprint.

But Ludacris's success has not been without controversy and struggle. His sometimes-raunchy lyrics and videos have drawn criticism from public figures, such as conservative media icon Bill O'Reilly. Hip-hop disputes with rivals including the rappers T.I. and Chingy have provided distractions and challenged his focus and determination.

Despite some setbacks, Ludacris has never let others' negativity get him down. While his earlier records were more lighthearted and outrageous, he has grown as an artist. Recently, he has covered more serious and socially minded subjects, such as drugs, relationships, and Hurricane Katrina, among others. He's also expanded his sound, while still giving longtime fans the catchy anthems they've come to expect.

With more than thirteen million albums sold, Ludacris is one of the most consistently successful artists and versatile hip-hop lyricists of the last decade. Not content to just rest on his laurels, he has also become a savvy media mogul. Most important, Ludacris has never forgotten his community or his fans. In 2001, he started the Ludacris Foundation (TLF) to help youth and families, especially in disadvantaged communities.

Though occasionally uninhibited and provocative, Ludacris is one of the good guys—a hard-working, determined, smart, savvy, talented musical artist and media personality with boundless energy and a big heart.

CHAPTER ONE

THE RISE OF CHRISTOPHER BRIDGES

Christopher Bridges was born to college students Roberta Shields and Wayne Brian Bridges in Champaign, Illinois, on September 11, 1977. From an early age, he loved music and performing and being the center of attention. "They [his parents] used to take me to college parties and let me get out in the middle of the floor and dance for all the other students," he told Sing365.com in 2007.

Like many youngsters, Chris loved sports, especially baseball, and wrestling. The one constant passion, however, was his love for music, especially

Ludacris poses for a photo with his mother, Roberta Shields, during the Ludacris Foundation's 5th Annual Dinner, on May 14, 2008, in Atlanta, Georgia.

hip-hop. Influenced by mid-1980s hip-hop legends like LL Cool J and Run-D.M.C., he tried his hand at rapping quite early. He told ConcertLiveWire.com in 2003, "Man, it was all 'bout music. I used to wake up every day listening to music that my parents would put on . . . I grew up on James Brown, Run-D.M.C., Fat Boys . . . I wrote my first rhyme when I was like nine years old. Then, I would do demo tape after demo tape . . . I loved the whole aspect of entertaining."

LUDACRIS: THE MEANING OF THE NAME

The name "Ludacris" is, of course, a play on the word "ludicrous." With his trademark wild afro, Ludacris has always displayed an outrageous style. His videos are innovative, fresh, and exciting, different from anything other rappers are creating. In his rap style, which varies on many tracks, he bends words and rhymes creatively, often with playful yells and hollers to punctuate certain lines. Asked about his name, he told MTV.com in 2007, "It kinda just describes me. Sometimes I have a split personality; sometimes I'm cool, calm, and collected. Other times I'm beyond crazy. My birth name is Chris, so it incorporates that."

A BUDDING PERFORMER

Writing and performing gave Chris a creative outlet. Since his family moved around frequently, and Chris never stayed in one school for long, hip-hop also provided a social network. Around the age of twelve, he had already joined his first rap crew, called the Loudmouth Hooligans. As he explained to MTV.com in an interview in 2007, he and his friends were heirs to the hip-hop tradition of having fun and being creative despite limited resources, coming up with music by "just beating on garbage cans, having people beatbox." Beatboxing is a form of vocal percussion, and it involves making rhythms by using your voice and mouth.

HOTLANTA: "BATTLING" IN THE LUNCHROOM

By the time Chris was thirteen years old, his family finally settled in Atlanta, Georgia, a longtime center of African American culture and commerce. Through the 1990s, Atlanta also grew as an epicenter of hip-hop, specifically southern hip-hop. With the rise of artists like OutKast, T.I., and Young Jeezy, southern hip-hop has grown in prominence in recent

Atlanta hip-hop heroes OutKast are pictured here receiving the Artist of the Year Award at the Source Hip-Hop Awards, in Los Angeles, California, in 1999.

years, rivaling the traditional East Coast/West Coast dominance of the genre.

Chris's outgoing personality blossomed early, as did his competitive streak. He started attending Banneker High School in Atlanta's College Park area and "battling" in the lunchroom. Battling is challenging others by freestyling, or inventing rhymes on the spot, daring your rivals to come up with better ones. Absorbed with battling, Chris often forgot to eat his lunch.

He was soon showing off his talents to the public at-large. Ludacris told MTV.com about his first show: "When I was like 13, I performed in a club in Atlanta. I took my shirt off, and everybody thought I was cute. I didn't have any muscles or nothing." His love for rapping only grew stronger, continuing through his time at Georgia State University (GSU), where he studied business and music management. It was then that he got his foot in the door of the music industry.

ON THE RADIO

After graduating high school and while attending GSU, Bridges landed an internship with Atlanta's urban radio station, Hot 97.5. There, he was known as DJ Chris Luva Luva. Though officially a producer, he became known for rapping on the promotional segments that ran during his late-night shift. Meanwhile, he was saving money and honing his skills. In time, his voice was as recognizable as those of the other DJs. As he told Sing365.com,

"I started rapping on the station promos. We did them over all of the top hits, so people got to hear me rap over tight beats." Soon enough, people began to take notice of this young talent.

A BIG BREAK

One of those people who pricked up their ears was the in-demand producer Timothy "Timbaland" Mosley. Timbaland had become famous producing songs for many hip-hop and R & B artists, such as Jay-Z, Missy Elliott, and Aaliyah. Timbaland contacted DJ Chris Luva Luva. They recorded together at the station, and the end result was "Phat Rabbit," which appeared on Timbaland's 1998 record, *Tim's Bio: Life from da Bassment*.

Superproducer Timbaland *(above)* played a crucial role in exposing a young Ludacris to a national audience.

DO IT YOURSELF

Around this time, other industry people became interested in Bridges, including famed producer Jermaine Dupri of So So

Def Records, who wanted to sign him. But Bridges's own DIY ("do it yourself") attitude won out. With money he had carefully saved, he formed his own independent label, Disturbing tha Peace (DTP), to put out his own record on his own terms. He would record under a new moniker that would soon make him famous: Ludacris.

Ludacris sold his debut album with little promotion. In fact, he sold many CDs for only seven dollars each from the trunk of his car. He later told MTV.com, "If you want something done right, you have to do it yourself. Putting something out independently is the best thing anyone can do . . . because you learn every aspect of the music game . . . When I put out [the album], it was a real struggle; I had to save up money to do everything, sell it out the trunk, and get it in the stores."

The response was overwhelming, given the modest marketing and distribution effort; as many as fifty thousand records were sold. The single "What's Your Fantasy?" was a minor hit in the southern hip-hop scene. This was a huge debut for an unknown, unsigned rapper, especially one without the promotional muscle of a major label behind him. That would soon change, however, because the debut album would quickly put Ludacris on the hip-hop map.

CHAPTER TWO

HITTING THE BIG TIME

For many years, New York City—the birthplace of hip-hop—and Los Angeles seemed to be the focal points of rap music. But the South had long had its own sound and rap legends. Early pioneers include Luther "Luke" Campbell, the driving force behind Florida's controversial but innovative 2 Live Crew. Other veterans include the Houston, Texas–based gangsta rappers the Geto Boys. One of the Geto Boys, Brad "Scarface" Jordan, gained further acclaim as one of the best MCs in the history of the game. In the late 1990s, Louisiana artists such as rapper/mogul

Master P and New Orleans' Hot Boys also enjoyed great success.

In the mid to late 1990s, Atlanta developed its own vibrant and diverse music scene, gaining a reputation as the Motown of the South, with several prominent labels, including Rowdy Records, So So Def, and LaFace Records. Atlanta spawned international superstars like Goodie Mob, Lil Jon, OutKast, Usher, TLC, and Toni Braxton. Locals often refer to their hometown as "the ATL" or "Hotlanta." Atlanta was at the forefront of what is widely called

Atlanta has long been a center of hip-hop and R & B. Stars such as Toni Braxton *(above)*, signed to Atlanta's LaFace Records, became household names.

Dirty South rap, a term first coined by Goodie Mob in 1995. The Dirty South sound is very club-oriented and energetic, with lyrical themes often centering on good times and demonstrating a distinctively southern cultural perspective.

Ludacris praises the Atlanta scene's sense of camaraderie. He told CNN in an October 2006 interview: "The one thing I hear when I go to different states is they love how much Atlanta artists stick together. It traces back to a culture where everyone knows there's enough room for everybody, and we all know we're stronger together than we are separate." Indeed, over the course of his career, Ludacris would appear on many local artists' tracks and vice versa.

DEF JAM SOUTH: A NEW LABEL, A NEW STAR

Russell Simmons, the New York–based hip-hop mogul who co-founded the famous Def Jam record label in the 1980s, hired the Geto Boys' Scarface to run the new southern division of his company, Def Jam South. One of Simmons's first priorities for Def Jam South was to sign Ludacris to the label.

Mogul Russell Simmons *(above)* started and runs Def Jam. Ludacris has praised him as a role model and inspiration.

For Ludacris, joining the same record label that had produced some of his favorite records as a youngster was a huge thrill. Simmons was also one of Ludacris's role models, having created a hip-hop empire that spanned music, a clothing line (Phat Farm), and other business ventures.

Ludacris later recalled to MTV.com that he was excited, despite the pressure of being the new label's first artist: "I felt that Def Jam has always been the number one hip-hop label. I love the way they market their artists. I felt if I was going to be the first artist signed to their Southern label, then they were going to put their all behind it." For Ludacris, it suddenly seemed that the sky was the limit.

BACK FOR THE FIRST TIME, THE SECOND TIME AROUND

By 2000, Ludacris was ready to take the world by storm. Def Jam South released his major-label debut, *Back for the First Time*, a rerecorded version of his first album, with five new songs. Hit-makers like Timbaland, the Neptunes, Jermaine Dupri, and Organized Noize produced some of the album's songs, with numerous guest stars providing verses.

The new version of "What's Your Fantasy?" and another single, "Southern Hospitality," ensured that Ludacris's first LP went platinum (selling at least a million copies) by December 2000. "What's Your Fantasy?" hit the Top 10 Singles chart in February 2001, and "Southern Hospitality" broke into the Top 40 the following month. At the age of twenty-three, Ludacris had an album on the Billboard Top 10 Albums chart.

GUEST STARRING: LUDACRIS

Hip-hop artists don't only put out their own albums and singles— they also frequently guest-star on other artists' tracks. Being in demand to supply guest verses is a clear sign of a rapper's skills and popularity.

Ludacris's guest spots have kept him in the public eye between releases of his own albums. In August 2001, riding on the popularity of his debut, he hit the Billboard Hip-Hop/R & B Singles chart for two weeks with a remix of Mariah Carey's hit "Loverboy," which also featured female rapper Da Brat. In September of that year, he joined Missy Elliott on one of her hit singles.

WORD OF MOUF

In November 2001, a little more than a year after *Back for the First Time* was released, Ludacris was ready to give his fans new material. Def Jam released his second album for the label, entitled *Word of Mouf*, earlier than planned after a few singles from the record were leaked to file-sharing networks like Napster.com. Many of the same producers had signed on for Ludacris's follow-up, among them Timbaland, Organized Noize, and Jermaine Dupri. The album yielded several hit singles, such as "Rollout (My Business)" and "Area Codes," which guest-starred rapper/producer Jazze Pha and West Coast artist Nate Dogg.

By January 2002, *Word of Mouf* went platinum, with "Rollout (My Business)" hitting the Top 40 by March and the Top 10 by April. Another Ludacris guest spot on Dupri's song "Welcome to Atlanta" made the Top 40. Soon enough, *Word of Mouf* was

certified double platinum. Even better, Ludacris's debut album was still selling; *Back for the First Time* went triple platinum in May 2002.

Industry recognition soon followed. *Back for the First Time* was nominated for the Grammy Award for Best Rap Album, and Ludacris and Nate Dogg were nominated for Best Rap/Sung Collaboration for "Area Codes."

Ludacris has stayed grounded in many ways, including keeping space in his schedule for hometown events. He is pictured here performing at the Music Midtown Festival in Atlanta.

STAYING GROUNDED

Anyone thrust into the spotlight of fame and fortune, especially within such a short period of time, must deal with unexpected challenges. Ludacris has done his best to remain grounded and positive, despite the newfound pressures and dramatic changes in his life.

One of the greatest challenges, he told Pseudo.com in an online interview, was the loss of privacy. Ludacris said one problem was "not being able to go a lot of places in public by yourself without getting mobbed." He insists that he always tries to be very nice to fans, but that someone interrupting him while he's eating dinner, for example, sometimes bothers him.

With his records selling well, Ludacris began to enjoy the good life. He could suddenly afford to have five cars, for instance. But his favorite car remained the ordinary one he had driven for years. In an interview with Hiphopdx.com in December 2007, he said, "I'm driving my 1993 Acura Legend as we speak! It does keep me grounded, man. Nobody really expects me to be driving this, but it's just the memory of who I was and where I was when all of this began that's most important to me. I don't really let a lot of this fame get to my head."

Success followed upon success in 2002. The single "Saturday (Ooh Ooh)" hit the Top 10 by summertime. Ludacris also received several MTV Video Music Award nominations, including Best Rap Video for "Saturday (Ooh Ooh)" and Best Video from a Film for "Area Codes," which had been featured in the movie *2 Fast 2 Furious*.

In October 2002, *Word of Mouf* went triple platinum. Not willing to simply bask in this glow, Ludacris started getting ready for his third Def Jam release (his fourth album overall). Yet, *Word of Mouf* continued to garner praise and attention. Over the following months, Ludacris received more award nods, including two Grammy nominations: one for *Word of Mouf* as Best Rap Album, and one for Best Rap Solo Performance, Male, for "Rollout (My Business)."

NEW HORIZONS

A natural lyricist and performer, Ludacris knew his wide-ranging talents weren't confined to making music. He was ambitious and saw that hip-hop moguls such as Russell Simmons, Jay-Z, and Sean "Diddy" Combs had used their musical careers as a platform from which to launch many different projects, including managing record labels, opening restaurants, making movies, and doing charity work.

Ludacris hoped to help other artists achieve the kind of success that he had by further developing his Disturbing tha Peace record label and production company. He also wanted to give back to the community, especially by supporting young people. In December 2001, he established the Ludacris Foundation (TLF) to do just that. As 2003 approached, he was ready to open all the doors available to him and invite as many people as possible to walk through them.

Ludacris is pictured here giving out Christmas presents to an Atlanta family during his annual Winter Wonderland Festival. It is one of many charity events he participates in through the Ludacris Foundation.

21

CHAPTER THREE
SUPERSTARDOM AND BEYOND

Since hip-hop first originated in the South Bronx in New York City in the late 1970s, it has courted controversy. Many mainstream critics have claimed that it glorifies violence, drugs, crime, and materialism, and that it degrades women. Artists as diverse as Public Enemy, 2 Live Crew, gangsta rap pioneer-turned-actor Ice-T, and many others have been attacked by politicians and pro-censorship groups. Ludacris is no exception. He has had several run-ins with prominent media critics over the content of his lyrics.

LUDACRIS VS. BILL O'REILLY

Ludacris's party anthems—
many of them admittedly quite
racy—have been natural targets
for critics of hip-hop music and
culture. On August 27, 2002,
popular conservative Fox
News talk show host Bill
O'Reilly harshly denounced
Ludacris's lyrics on his show,
The O'Reilly Factor.

O'Reilly was especially
angry that PepsiCo, the maker
of Pepsi Cola, was using
Ludacris as a spokesperson.
He told his viewers, "I'm

Conservative media personality Bill O'Reilly *(above)* sparked controversy and boycotts of Pepsi when he criticized Ludacris's music and lyrics and called for the soft-drink company to drop him as a spokesman.

calling for all responsible Americans to fight back and punish
Pepsi for using a man who degrades women, who encourages
substance abuse, and does all the things that hurt particularly
the poor in our society . . . I'm calling for all Americans to say,
'Hey, Pepsi, I'm not drinking your stuff.'" O'Reilly later back-
tracked, claiming he had never explicitly called for a boycott.

Pepsi soon responded by dropping Ludacris, hiring instead
heavy metal artist Ozzy Osbourne and his family, who were

then stars of a popular reality-TV show documenting their comically dysfunctional family dynamics. Soon, Def Jam head Russell Simmons jumped into action, organizing his own boycott against Pepsi for dropping Ludacris. He insisted upon an apology from Pepsi. He also demanded that the corporation donate millions of dollars to his Hip-Hop Summit Action Network, a nonprofit organization devoted to the empowerment of youth through education and involvement in hip-hop culture. Pepsi agreed to the latter, but it never formally apologized.

For Ludacris, Simmons, and many hip-hop fans, replacing Ludacris with the Obsournes was hypocritical. Ozzy Osbourne's career, including his reality show, had been controversial, too. His musical and stage persona are associated with Satanism and the occult, and he and members of his family have had well-documented drug problems. Many fans saw a double standard at work, one that demonized hip-hop while giving a free pass to other popular musical genres that were no less provocative. Ludacris told Pseudo.com, "I think they used me as an example . . . I think they were attacking hip-hop as a whole."

LUDACRIS'S THIRD DEF JAM ALBUM

On his third record, Ludacris employed the same winning formula of clever, funny raps. Yet, he also decided to branch out into new, darker lyrical themes. Talking about the upcoming album, he told CreativeLoafing.com, "People are going to hear some of the stuff that made them listen to me in the first place . . . But I also take things the extra step. I talk about subjects no one would expect me to talk about. They'll see a serious side, talking about hard times."

Still, Ludacris recognized that you don't radically change a winning formula, even if you want to grow artistically. He continued, "You don't want to suddenly change everything you do . . . You throw in three or four songs to see if you can go that extra step. At least if it goes wrong, you know you still have your basis there." He also told ConcertLiveWire.com in a March 2003 interview: "My rap is always moving in a new direction, and it always will be."

Ludacris's combination of caution and risk-taking paid off. His third album for Def Jam was a big success, selling 429,000 copies in the United States in its first week.

LUDACRIS VS. T.I.

Atlanta rappers tend to stick together. But the rivalry between Clifford "T.I." Harris and Ludacris threatened to spin out of control. The beef became public when the two worked on "Stomp," a song by Young Buck on which they each recorded verses that insulted the other. T.I.'s verse was later taken off the record, replaced by one from The Game.

In response, on T.I.'s song "You Know What It Is," he seemed to express his jealousy of Ludacris, who had beaten

After a well-publicized beef, Ludacris performed with rival T.I. at BET's Welcome to Atlanta Jam. Onstage, it seemed that the two rappers had reconciled.

him out for a Grammy Award in 2004 (for "Yeah," a collaboration with Usher and Lil John): "Had the album of the year . . . Grammy or not!" In true battle rap fashion, Ludacris responded with a remix of 50 Cent's "I Get Money," in which he declared his supremacy. Rappers often battle each other via songs, seeking to maintain their "street cred" (street credibility).

Playfully rapped insults soon turned into something darker, however, as tensions between T.I. and Ludacris escalated. T.I. scuffled with Chaka Zulu, a co-owner of Disturbing tha Peace, before a Black Entertainment Television (BET) event in Los Angeles in June 2007. However, T.I. apologized at the BET Awards a week later, declaring onstage, "I would just say that it was very unfortunate and very inappropriate."

Things seemingly have cooled down. The rappers later teamed up in a public appearance for Atlanta's V-103 radio

WHERE'S THE BEEF?

The music industry, especially the hip-hop scene, is very competitive. A popular hip-hop performer can easily make enemies. Rivalries between rappers range from friendly verbal sparring on competing album tracks to very real, even deadly, violence. It is widely suspected, for example, that both Christopher "Notorious B.I.G." Wallace and Tupac "2Pac" Shakur, both murdered in the late 1990s, died as a result of fallout from a prolonged East Coast/West Coast "rap war." Conflict between rappers, whether individuals or groups, is often referred to as "beef."

station in October 2007, and they have been acting friendly at other public events since.

A FALLING OUT WITH CHINGY

One of Ludacris's favorite things is helping up-and-coming performers. He has invited many lesser-known local rappers in Atlanta to guest-star on his tracks, especially those signed to Disturbing tha Peace. One artist he signed was Chingy, a rapper from St. Louis, Missouri, who rose to popularity partly from his association with fellow St. Louis superstar Nelly.

Ludacris appeared on Chingy's single "Holidae In," along with Snoop Dogg, helping propel Chingy's *Jackpot* LP to great

success. Soon, however, Chingy had left the label following a dispute over royalties with his manager, Chaka Zulu, complaining publicly about the disagreement in the pages of the hip-hop magazine *XXL*. Ludacris told MTV.com in November 2004, "This is the first time we hear about his accusations . . . so all respect is lost. He keeps saying it's cool. It's not cool . . . It's completely over."

Ludacris and Zulu insisted that Chingy's lawyers and accountants had confirmed that Chingy had not been shortchanged in any way. Chingy's story began to change somewhat when he also began to say that he left the label because he needed to grow artistically and expand his career beyond DTP. Ludacris countered this new claim by insisting that helping fellow artists was his priority. "I sign artists with the expectation of every single artist being as big as they can possibly be . . . You can still internally do your own thing, but still be a part of the

After signing Chingy *(above left)* to his DTP label, Ludacris *(right)* experienced some disagreements with the young rapper, but they later made up and worked with each other again.

family. No one's going to pigeonhole you . . . We're here to make you as successful as possible because it in turn makes us successful."

In a bit of a twist, Chingy surprised many when he actually returned to the DTP label in 2007 and resumed working with Ludacris. On a track called "Make That Money," Chingy rhymed, "Was gone for a minute, back with the crew/Who?/DTP, so if you top, we came to move you." It seemed to be a return to the family atmosphere that Ludacris had always encouraged.

CHAPTER FOUR
THE ACTOR, THE MOGUL, THE LEGACY

Ludacris doesn't limit himself to music or music videos when it comes to being onscreen. While many hip-hoppers, such as Ice-T and Ice Cube, have made a successful transition to films and television, acting isn't for everyone. Despite the common perception that rappers are boastful and egotistical, Ludacris approaches acting with humility, patience, and drive.

A "CRASH" COURSE IN THE MOVIE INDUSTRY

Ludacris's first major role was as Tej, an ex-street racer in the urban car-chase film *2 Fast 2 Furious*. But perhaps the greatest learning experience, and most well-received role, for the budding young rapper-turned-actor was in 2005's *Crash*, a hard-hitting drama about race relations in Los Angeles that was directed and cowritten by Paul Haggis.

This still photo from the 2005 film *Crash* shows Ludacris with his costar Larenz Tate *(left)*. The two played carjackers whose actions lead them in unexpected directions.

Surrounded by accomplished actors—Matt Dillon, Brendan Fraser, Sandra Bullock, Terrence Howard, and Don Cheadle, among many others—Ludacris knew he had to step up his game. Taking a lesson from his video work, it was time to transform himself into another person entirely once the cameras began rolling.

LEARNING THE ROPES

"Since I was the freshman of the group," he explained in a May 2005 article in the *San Francisco Chronicle*, "I basically wanted to soak it all in and learn from these great actors . . . Once I heard all the people were going to be a part of it, man, I knew I had to step up to the plate because I was the least experienced actor in it." *Crash* producer Cathy Schulman and coproducer Don Cheadle, however, were impressed with Ludacris's potential. "As soon as Don saw that first raw tape [of Ludacris reading for his role], he said it doesn't matter if he's losing lines or this and that, this guy is a star," Schulman told the *San Francisco Chronicle*.

The results were overwhelmingly positive. Ludacris received good reviews for his role as an intelligent, complicated carjacker. He would appear in another major film, the inspirational hip-hop drama *Hustle & Flow*, also released in 2005. In it, he played a rapper visiting his hometown of Memphis who had let stardom go to his head.

At the 2006 Academy Awards, Ludacris was in an enviable position: two movies he had worked on were up for Oscars. *Hustle & Flow* was nominated for several awards, while *Crash* was a huge underdog in the Best Picture category. Ludacris was riding high already because *Crash* had won a Screen Actors Guild (SAG) Award for best cast, and a Critics' Choice Award for best acting ensemble. He told MTV.com, "I'm thrilled that a film so raw and honest had been recognized. To be part of such a talented cast like this comes once in a lifetime, if it ever comes at all." The icing on the cake, however, was when *Crash* became the surprise Oscar winner for Best Picture.

IN HIS OWN WORDS

On acting: "[The] difference between breaking through or not breaking through is how serious we take it. Studying the craft, working on your role, being humble and not thinking you know everything, and coming into it as a student, all of that has a lot to do with it."
—HipHopDx.com

On hip-hop role models: "Russell Simmons is the man who laid the blueprint for anyone else I would probably name. I really look up to him. His business sense, how humble he is, and his desire to give back and acknowledge his responsibility here on Earth is extremely impressive."
—HipHopDx.com

On family: "My daughter [Karma] cracks me up all the time; she's five years old, and she makes me laugh all the time. I learn things from her every day. I learn more from her than she does from me. I was a kid who had a kid, and she made me a grown-up."
—CNN.com, October 2006

On being professional: "If you get there early or on time, you can get as much information as possible and you can finish meetings on time or even ahead of schedule. Timeliness shows people that you are professional, and it maintains and grows relationships."
—Daveyd.com

A NEW DIRECTION

While jump-starting his film and television career, Ludacris was still making music and promoting his label's artists. On his newer records, he was expanding his lyrical themes to address important and serious issues in his life and career.

One single from Ludacris's third Def Jam album was "Blow It Out," a track that addressed his public dispute with Bill O'Reilly. It was a precursor to his upcoming fourth Def Jam record, which would be less lighthearted and party-oriented on some tracks.

Ludacris's new album was released on December 7, 2004, debuting at number one. It sold 322,000 units its first week. Along with guest spots by DTP artists like Small World, Bobby Valentino, and Dolla Boy, there were also verses from rappers Nas, DMX, Sleepy Brown, and old-school legend Doug E. Fresh, among others.

RELEASE THERAPY: A NEW SOUND, A NEW LOOK

In 2006, fans were eagerly awaiting Ludacris's newest record, *Release Therapy*. Released as a CD, Ludacris wanted it to mimic old-school mixtapes, which were double sided. One half would focus on "Release," which would express his frustration with various social issues. The other half would be "Therapy," in the form of feel-good party anthems.

Pharrell Williams of the Neptunes production team appeared on the single "Money Maker" with Ludacris; the single was released ahead of the album in July 2006. Another song, "Runaway Love," which was about teen runaways, propelled the album to number one on the charts, with more than 300,000 copies sold in the week after its release on September 26, 2006. Other weighty subjects addressed on the album included fatherhood, the tragedy of Hurricane Katrina, and Ludacris's spiritual side.

Ludacris performs onstage at the MGM Grand Garden Arena in Las Vegas, Nevada, as part of the Billboard Awards. That night, he and Pharrell Williams of the Neptunes performed "Money Maker" together.

After years of his trademark look—a wild afro or cornrow braids—Ludacris celebrated the appearance of *Release Therapy* by cutting his hair into a neater "fade" haircut. "This album that's coming out is so different than all the material that I've recorded over the past four albums, that I needed to complement the new sound with a new look," he told the Associated Press in August 2006. He added, "It's a lot of things that I'm speaking on that I've never talked about. I felt like people knew who Ludacris was, but people never knew who Chris Bridges was."

GIVING BACK, UP CLOSE AND PERSONAL

Ludacris is not only an outrageous showman and a serious actor. He has also been showing his generous side for years. He established the Ludacris Foundation (TLF) in 2001 with the aim of, in the words of the organization's motto, "helping youth help themselves." Rather than simply contributing money to other organizations' projects, he took his traditional hands-on, do-it-yourself approach to philanthropy. He was inspired to directly help youth and families, especially those in the poorer communities that Ludacris himself had at times found himself in while growing up.

According to TLF's Web site, it promotes the qualities, skills, and activities that Ludacris felt had helped him succeed: "self-esteem, spirituality, communication, education, leadership, goal setting, physical activity, and community service." TLF does everything from providing holiday meals to needy families and teaching youngsters about hygiene and healthy eating, to hosting celebrity benefits for the HIV-positive and partnering with organizations such as United Cerebral Palsy to help disabled youth. The foundation has gained praise for this community-based work.

In a May 2003 interview on Daveyd.com, Ludacris stressed that TLF was involved in many different projects. "We go to different cities and are careful to not just focus on one thing. We want to do a lot of stuff." Ludacris also told Pseudo.com that an important part of TLF for him was actually going to meet youth and trying to inspire them personally. That's why he takes the time to help feed hungry families, pay visits to hospitalized children, and give motivational speeches at schools. "They see me on television a lot, but it's even more important to go and see people face-to-face," he said.

LUDACRIS: RESTAURATEUR

One of Ludacris's many dreams was to one day own his own restaurant. To make this dream a reality, he combined his keen business sense with that of veteran restaurateur Chris Yeo, owner of the Straits chain of Singaporean eateries in California. Ludacris bought a building in downtown Atlanta and, after investing one million dollars in renovations, launched the first of several planned Straits locations in April 2008.

Ludacris and Yeo met at a TLF event, forming a friendship over their shared passion for charity work. Eventually, they decided to become business partners. As with anything Ludacris does, though, his new restaurant added a unique twist: the cuisine is an unlikely mix of Singaporean and down-home southern cuisine.

For Ludacris, the attention to detail and work involved in getting a restaurant off the ground was, as always, a valuable learning experience. "It's been extremely intense," he told SundayPaper.com. "One thing it's done is taught me . . . a lot of patience. It's been a year in the making . . . I just think if you're going to do something right, it does take time."

TRIUMPH AND TRAGEDY

In February 2007, Ludacris stood in triumph on the stage at the Grammy Awards. That evening, he had won two awards: one for Best Rap Album for *Release Therapy*, and one for Best Rap Song for "Money Maker." Despite finally being recognized by the Grammys after years of hard work, he had something else on his mind while onstage: his ailing father, who had helped expose him to music at a young age.

"Wayne Brian Bridges, I love you to death," he told the audience, dedicating his Best Rap Album Award to his father. Not long after, on February 25, 2007, the elder Bridges passed away at the age of fifty-two. Friends, fellow musicians, and fans all sent their support, and Ludacris graciously thanked everyone for their good wishes during a tough time.

LOOKING AHEAD: HERE TO STAY

Even after more than a decade in the hip-hop game, Ludacris remains ever watchful and ready for his next big move. His highly anticipated *Theater of the Mind* album was prepared for a fall 2008 release. He considered it his most ambitious album yet. It was named for the theatrical experience he hopes to impart to listeners. "It's basically somewhat like a motion-picture album," he told SundayPaper.com in April 2008. "The way the songs flow into each other, they have great concepts to them . . . It plays out like a movie."

With multiplatinum success, a bright future in Hollywood, and profitable businesses and philanthropy keeping him busy, Ludacris is not slowing down at all. CreativeLoafing.com asked him in October 2003 whether his non-musical projects were a way to guarantee continued success, given the hip-hop world's ever-changing tastes and trends. "I feel like I'm going to be in music all my life," he said. "Even if I'm writing stuff for people, that's still me being in music . . . I just want to leave something for this world of hip-hop. I

Ludacris is shown displaying the Grammy Awards he won for Best Rap Song for "Money Maker" and Best Rap Album for *Release Therapy*.

want to be known as the most versatile MC. . . It scares me when I see other people disappearing so quickly, but I kind of see how it happens. Sometimes, it's the choices they make in their lives. Not everybody has the same goals. Some people want to stop after four albums or something. But I want to be able to stay."

If energy, determination, wild creativity, and pure heart have anything to do with success, Ludacris will be able to go wherever he wants and stay for as long as he wants. His ludicrous brand of talent and industry is built to last.

TIMELINE

1977 September 11, Christopher "Ludacris" Bridges is born in Champaign, Illinois.

2000 Ludacris forms Disturbing tha Peace Records (DTP) to independently release his debut record, which becomes a regional hit and makes industry figures take notice of this rising talent; Def Jam releases Ludacris's major-label debut, *Back for the First Time*; *Back for the First Time* is certified platinum, and the single "What's Your Fantasy?" hits the Top 40 chart.

2001 Ludacris and DTP co-owner Chaka Zulu form the charitable organization the Ludacris Foundation (TLF); Ludacris and Da Brat strike it big when their remix of Mariah Carey's "Loverboy" remains on the Billboard R & B/Hip-Hop Singles charts for two weeks; Ludacris's follow-up album, *Word of Mouf*, is released to great commercial success.

2002 *Word of Mouf* goes platinum, and the single "Rollout (My Business)" makes it into the Top 40.

2003 Ludacris releases his third Def Jam album.

2004 Ludacris's fourth Def Jam album is released and goes on to sell 322,000 copies in its first week.

2005 Ludacris plays rapper Skinny Black in the inspirational hip-hop drama *Hustle & Flow*.

2006 The movie *Crash* is released, costarring Ludacris, who also appears on several episodes of *Law and Order: Special Victims Unit*; his fifth album, *Release Therapy*, sells 300,000 copies in its first week.

2007 Ludacris wins two Grammy Awards; his father, Wayne Brian Bridges, dies.

2008 Ludacris opens a restaurant in Atlanta with business partner Chris Yeo.

SELECTED DISCOGRAPHY

2000   *Back for the First Time* (Def Jam)
2001   *Word of Mouf* (Def Jam)
2005   *Ludacris Presents: Disturbing tha Peace* (Compilation with DTP Artists) (Disturbing tha Peace/Def Jam)
2006   *Release Therapy* (Disturbing tha Peace/Def Jam)

GLOSSARY

battle A freestyling contest among two or more rappers.

beatboxing A form of vocal percussion that is part of hip-hop culture, in which rhythms are produced by the mouth and voice.

beef A disagreement between two individuals or groups. Hip-hop beef may be limited to simply disparaging your rival on record, or it can escalate into more serious tension and a potentially violent conflict.

demo A sample of a rapper or other musician's music, recorded to market oneself to record labels, producers, or venues, often in hopes of performing or signing a record deal.

DIY Stands for "do it yourself," which describes how rappers and other artists create and distribute their own art, without the help of a major corporation.

DJ Short for "disc jockey." In hip-hop, it refers to the person who provides the music that backs hip-hop lyrics, usually with two sets of turntables, and, more recently, with digital media.

freestyling Improvising raps and performing them with little or no lyrics prepared ahead of time.

gangsta Refers to hardcore hip-hop in which the lyrics deal with gang life and crime, including violence, drug dealing, and other aspects of a harsh urban landscape.

hardcore A harder, more aggressive form of hip-hop, with more serious lyrics and darker and more minimal beats.

MC Traditionally stands for "master of ceremonies," but within the world of hip-hop, it more often means "microphone controller."

mixtape In hip-hop, a collection of songs by an artist or artists mixed together, though often with a single rapper performing verses and freestyling over remixes and collaborations. Mixtapes are often recorded and released to build a rapper's popularity.

mogul A businessperson who has reached the highest administrative and ownership level in a particular industry or set of industries.

R & B Short for "rhythm and blues," it currently refers to a contemporary form of African American music that incorporates soul, funk, dance, and, most recently, hip-hop.

remix In hip-hop and other African American music, this is a rerecording of a song with new verses and/or music, sometimes with different artists guest-starring on particular tracks.

FOR MORE INFORMATION

Def Jam Recordings
825 Eighth Avenue
New York, NY 10019
Web site: http://www.defjam.com
This is home to Ludacris's record label, and it remains one of the most prolific distributors of hip-hop music.

The Ludacris Foundation (TLF)
3645 Market Place Boulevard, Suite 130-318
East Point, GA 30344-5747
(202) 365-5401
Web site: http://www.theludacrisfoundation.org
TLF spearheads projects to help youth and families nationwide.

WEB SITES

Due to the changing nature of Internet links, Rosen Publishing has developed an online list of Web sites related to the subject of this book. This site is updated regularly. Please use this link to access the list:

http://www.rosenlinks.com/lhhb/luda

FOR FURTHER READING

Abrams, Dennis. *Beastie Boys* (Hip-Hop Stars). New York, NY: Chelsea House, 2007.

Abrams, Dennis. *Jay-Z* (Hip-Hop Stars). New York, NY: Checkmark Books, 2007.

Bankston, John. *Missy Elliott: Hip-Hop Superstars* (Blue Banner Biographies). Hockessin, DE: Mitchell Lane Publishers, 2004.

Burns, Kate. *Rap Music and Culture* (Current Controversies). Farmington Hills, MI: Greenhaven Press, 2008.

Hatch, Thomas. *A History of Hip-Hop: The Roots of Rap* (High Five Reading). Bloomington, MN: Red Brick Learning, 2005.

Lommel, Cookie. *Russell Simmons* (Hip-Hop Stars). New York, NY: Chelsea House, 2007.

Merino, Noel. *Rap Music* (Introducing Issues with Opposing Viewpoints). Farmington Hills, MI: Greenhaven Press, 2008.

Scott, Celia. *Ludacris* (Hip-Hop). Broomall, PA: Mason Crest Publishers, 2007.

Waters, Rosa. *Hip-Hop: A Short History* (Hip-Hop). Broomall, PA: Mason Crest Publishers, 2007.

BIBLIOGRAPHY

Associated Press. "Ludacris Loses Braids, Gains a New Sound: Rapper Displays a More Mature Side on His New Album 'Release Therapy.'" August 3, 2006. Retrieved May 2008 (http://www.msnbc.msn.com/id/14169288).

Hart, Hugh. "Ludacris' Crash Course in Acting." *San Francisco Chronicle*, May 8, 2005. Retrieved May 2008 (http://www.sfgate.com/cgi-bin/article.cgi?f=/c/a/2005/05/08/PKGF6CGNK21.DTL&type=movies).

Landrum Jr., Jonathan. "Ludacris Returns to His Alma Mater in Atlanta." MSN.com, May 13, 2008. Retrieved May 2008 (https://www.music.msn.com/news/article.aspx?news=313936).

Love, B. "Ludacris: Standing Bridges." HipHopDx.com, December 17, 2007. Retrieved May 2008 (http://www.hiphopdx.com/index/features/id.973/title.ludacris-standing-bridges/p.1).

Reid, Shaheem, and Bridget Bland. "T.I. Regrets Scuffle with Ludacris' Manager, Says LP Is 'Best Hip-Hop Has to Offer.'" MTV.com, July 2, 2007. Retrieved May 2008 (http://www.mtv.com/news/articles/1563805/20070629/t_i_.jhtml).

Sarig, Roni. *Third Coast: OutKast, Timberland, and How Hip-Hop Became a Southern Thing.* Cambridge, MA: Perseus Books, 2007.

INDEX

ABOUT THE AUTHOR

Philip Wolny is a writer, editor, and masters' student of Euroculture who lives in Kraków, Poland. Before going overseas, he spent most of his formative years in New York City, where he witnessed firsthand hip-hop morphing from old school, to the golden age of hip-hop, to gritty mid-1990s street rap, to the widely varying styles of today. In writing this book, he gained a newfound admiration for Ludacris as an artist and human being. Wolny's previous work in the Hip-Hop Biographies series for Rosen was a volume on Sean "Diddy" Combs.

PHOTO CREDITS